Oh-So-Easy Jewelry

Slide some flashy beads on a basic chain bracelet or necklace. Add charms to a bracelet of strappy leather or knotted cord. Use leftover beads to create dangly matching earrings. This book shows how easy it is to create unique jewelry in an instant from plain chains, links, closures, loose beads, and other findings.

2

4

6

8

10

12

14

14

16

18

18

20
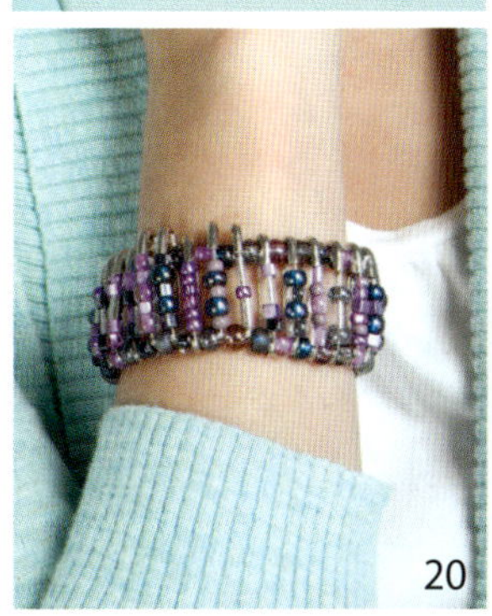
20

22

24

26

26

26

28

30

LEISURE ARTS, INC. • Maumelle, Arkansas

Slider Pendants

These necklaces are oh-so-fast and easy to make. Once you make the pendants, just slide them on pre-made chain or multi-cord necklaces. To get lots of bang for your buck, purchase one or two chains then make multiple pendants using different colors and types of beads. Mix and match the pendants and necklaces to have a "new" piece of jewelry for every outfit!

SHOPPING LIST

- ☐ assorted large (approx.14-20mm) beads (we used 1 per pendant)
- ☐ assorted small and medium (approx. 6-10mm) beads (we used 1-3 per pendant)
- ☐ assorted seed and bugle beads (we used 3-4 per pendant)
- ☐ medium/large round or square jump rings
- ☐ head pins
- ☐ pre-made chain or multi-cord necklaces
- ☐ wire cutters
- ☐ chain-nose pliers (2 pair) and round-nose pliers

To make each Necklace:

1. Beginning with a seed or small bead, use assorted beads and a head pin to make a bead dangle (page 32) that is approximately 1 3/4" long.

2. To make the pendant, attach a jump ring (page 31) to the bead dangle. Slide the pendant on your necklace.

Glittered Bezel Jewelry

SHOPPING LIST

- ☐ Mod Podge® Dimensional Magic™
- ☐ very fine glitter
- ☐ metal jewelry piece with a bezel or bezels (cuff, ring, or bracelet)
- ☐ stand to hold ring or cuff upright while they dry (this could be 2 books placed side-by-side, a vise, or a block of Styrofoam™)

To make Glittered Bezel Jewelry:

1. If making a ring or cuff, place the piece upright in your stand *(Fig. 1)*. Lay the bracelet on a flat surface.

Fig. 1

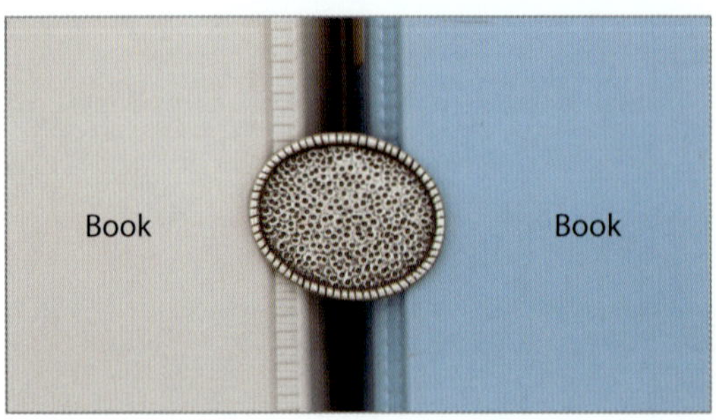

2. Fill the bezel(s) with Dimensional Magic *(Fig. 2)*.

Fig. 2

3. Sprinkle glitter on the Dimensional Magic *(Fig. 3)*. Allow to dry for at least 24 hours. ***Note:*** As Dimensional Magic dries, it may shrink leaving a sunken area in the center of the bezel.

Fig. 3

4. Fill in any sunken areas with more Dimensional Magic and glitter and allow to dry for at least 24 hours.

Connector Necklaces

DANGLES AND CHARMS CHAIN NECKLACE

SHOPPING LIST

- ☐ 18" silver chain necklace with a lobster clasp
- ☐ silver branch connector
- ☐ silver charm and bead dangle assortment
- ☐ silver jump rings
- ☐ wire cutters
- ☐ chain-nose pliers (2 pair)

To make the Necklace:

1. Use jump rings (page 31) to attach the charms and bead dangles to the connector.
2. Use the wire cutters to cut the necklace in half at the center front.
3. Use jump rings to attach one chain end to each end of the connector.

DANGLE AND CHARM RIBBON NECKLACE

SHOPPING LIST

- ☐ 60" of 1/4" wide ribbon
- ☐ silver branch connector
- ☐ silver charm
- ☐ bead dangle
- ☐ silver jump rings
- ☐ chain-nose pliers (2 pair)

To make the Necklace:

1. Use jump rings (page 31) to attach the charm and the bead dangle to the connector.
2. Cut the ribbon into two 30" lengths.
3. Thread a ribbon length through one end loop on the connector; fold the ribbon in half. Thread the ribbon ends through a jump ring; slide the ring down the ribbon to the fold.
4. Repeat Step 3 to attach the remaining ribbon length to the opposite end of the connector.

laugh

Tubes, Beads, & Cord Necklaces & Earrings

Satin cord, bead dangles, and silver tubes combine to make these super fast necklaces. Add a pair of beaded earrings for lots of "wow" with very little effort!

BLUE NECKLACE AND EARRINGS

SHOPPING LIST

- ☐ silver curved tube with attached loops
- ☐ large flat faceted blue bead
- ☐ 2 medium flat faceted blue beads
- ☐ 2 medium round faceted blue beads
- ☐ 3 small round faceted blue beads
- ☐ 2mm satin cord
- ☐ 2 1/2" long pieces of silver chain
- ☐ silver jump rings
- ☐ silver lobster clasp
- ☐ silver foldover cord ends
- ☐ silver ear wires
- ☐ silver head pins
- ☐ silver eye pins
- ☐ wire cutters
- ☐ chain-nose pliers (2 pair) and round-nose pliers

To make the Necklace:

1. Make 2 bead dangles (page 32) with the 2 medium round faceted blue beads and head pins. Use jump rings (page 31) to attach the bead dangles to the outer loops of the tube.

2. Make a large bead dangle with the large bead and a head pin.

3. Make a bead connector (page 32) with a small bead and an eye pin *(Fig. 1)*.

Fig. 1

4. Attach the connector to the large bead dangle to make the pendant. Use a jump ring to attach the pendant to the center loop of the tube.

5. Slide the tube onto the cord and attach the foldover cord ends (page 31). Use jump rings to attach the clasp to the cord ends.

To make the Earrings:

1. Make 2 small bead dangles (page 32) with the small beads and head pins.
2. Make 2 bead connectors with the medium flat beads and eye pins *(Fig. 2)*.

Fig. 2

3. Use a jump ring to attach one end of each chain piece to an ear wire. Attach a connector to the remaining end of each chain piece. Attach a bead dangle to each connector.

Continued on page 10.

PINK NECKLACE

SHOPPING LIST

- ☐ silver curved tube with attached loops
- ☐ assorted small, med, and large pink acrylic beads
- ☐ 2mm satin cord
- ☐ silver jump rings
- ☐ silver lobster clasp
- ☐ silver foldover cord ends
- ☐ silver head pins
- ☐ wire cutters
- ☐ chain-nose pliers and round-nose pliers
- ☐ jeweler's glue

To make the Necklace:

1. Make 3 large bead, 3 medium bead, and 9 small bead dangles (page 32) with 1 bead on each dangle.

2. Referring to **Fig. 1**, attach 1 medium and 2 small bead dangles to a jump ring (page 31) .

Fig. 1

3. Attach 1 large and 1 small bead dangle to a jump ring *(Fig. 2)*.

Fig. 2

4. Join the 2 jump rings *(Fig. 3)*.

Fig. 3

5. Attach 1 of the joined jump rings to a loop on the tube.

6. Repeat Steps 2-4 to make and attach 2 more bead dangles.

7. Cut a piece of satin cord your desired necklace length. Slide the tube on the cord.

8. Attach a foldover cord end to each end of the necklace (page 31). Use jump rings to attach the clasp to the cord ends

Leather Bracelets

CUFF BRACELET WITH CHAIN

SHOPPING LIST

- ☐ leather cuff bracelet with pre-punched holes
- ☐ 1.5mm round leather cord
- ☐ two 5" chain lengths
- ☐ craft glue

To make the Bracelet:

1. Cut two 20" lengths of cord. Referring to Fig. 1 and leaving a 2" tail, thread the cord ends from front to back through the second holes on one end of the bracelet. **Note:** *For clarity, the leather cord is shown in two colors.*

Fig. 1

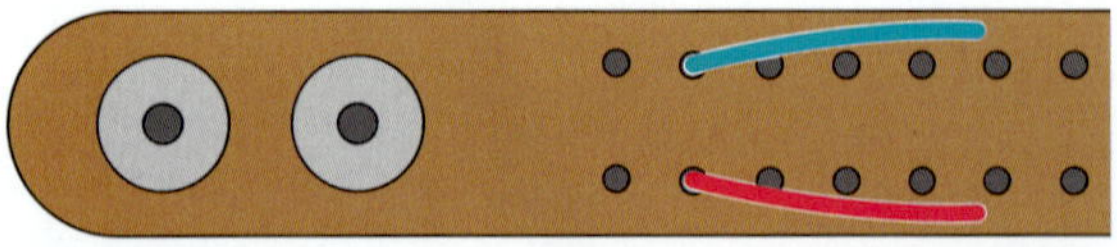

2. On the front of the bracelet, make an "X" with the cord *(Fig. 2)*.

Fig. 2

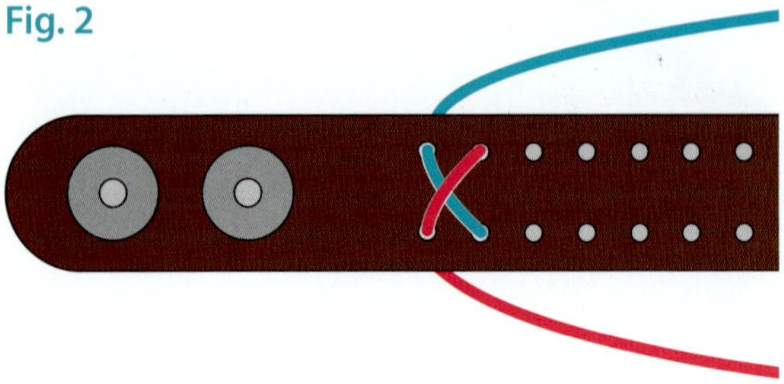

3. Use the right cord to attach a chain length along the right bracelet edge. Starting back at the begining end, use the left cord to attach the remaining chain length along the left bracelet edge *(Fig. 3)*.

Fig. 3

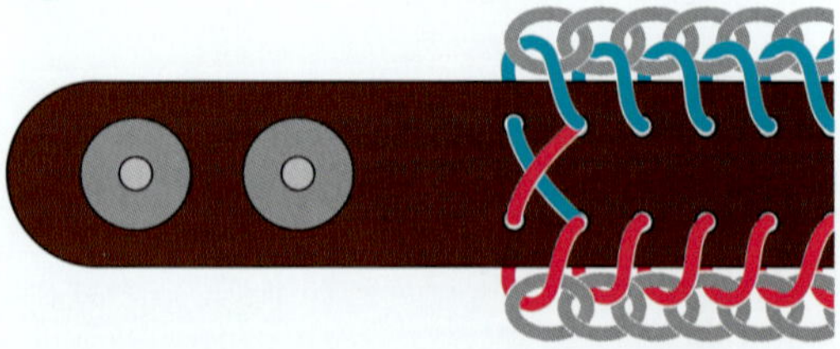

4. When you reach the end of the bracelet, make an "X" on the front with the cord ends and bring the cord ends to the back of the bracelet.

5. On the back, tie the cord ends together; trim the cord ends. Tuck the ends under the loops on the back and glue in place *(Fig. 4)*. Repeat on beginning end of the bracelet.

Fig. 4

WOVEN BRACELET WITH CHARMS

SHOPPING LIST

- ☐ pre-made adjustable woven leather bracelet
- ☐ assorted antique silver charms (we used 7)
- ☐ large silver jump rings
- ☐ chain-nose pliers (2 pair)

To make the Bracelet:

Use the jump rings (page 31) to attach the charms to the leather cords on the bracelet.

Medallion Necklaces

LEATHER NECKLACE

SHOPPING LIST

- ☐ 18" long pre-made leather necklace with attached antique brass jump rings and clasp
- ☐ 2 antique brass muse tokens
- ☐ 1" square antique brass bezel
- ☐ clear glass jewelry tile to fit bezel
- ☐ cardstock
- ☐ Mod Podge® Dimensional Magic™
- ☐ chain-nose pliers (2 pair)

To make the Necklace:

1. From your computer, print a letter that fits your bezel on cardstock .
2. Coat the back of the tile with Dimensional Magic. Center the tile over the letter and gently press in place; allow to dry completely.
3. Trim away the excess cardstock. Use Dimensional Magic to glue the tile in the bezel; allow to dry.
4. Use jump rings (page 31) from the necklace to attach the tokens and bezel to the necklace.

CHAIN NECKLACE

SHOPPING LIST

- ☐ 18" long pre-made black chain necklace
- ☐ 1" square black bezel
- ☐ clear glass jewelry tile to fit bezel
- ☐ 2 pre-made bead dangles
- ☐ 2 black jump rings
- ☐ cardstock
- ☐ Mod Podge® Dimensional Magic™
- ☐ chain-nose pliers (2 pair)

To make the Necklace:

1. From your computer, print a graphic design that fits your bezel on cardstock.
2. Coat the back of the tile with Dimensional Magic. Center the tile over the design and gently press in place; allow to dry completely.
3. Trim away the excess cardstock. Use Dimensional Magic to glue the tile in the bezel; allow to dry.
4. Use a jump ring (page 31) to attach the bezel to the necklace.
5. Attach the bead dangles to the remaining jump ring and then attach that jump ring to the bezel jump ring.

WONDERFUL
COURAGEOUS

Memory Wire Bracelets

AQUA GLASS BRACELET

SHOPPING LIST

- ☐ memory wire
- ☐ assorted small aqua glass beads (we used approx. 70 beads)
- ☐ medium aqua glass beads (we used 8)
- ☐ 2 silver charms
- ☐ 2 jump rings
- ☐ memory wire shears
- ☐ chain-nose pliers (2 pair) and round-nose pliers

To make the Bracelet:

1. Wrap the memory wire around your wrist 2-3 times to determine bracelet length. Use the memory wire shears to cut a piece of wire this length. Make a loop at one wire end (page 32).

2. Thread the beads on the wire as desired. Make a loop at the remaining wire end.

3. Use a jump ring (page 31) to add a charm to the loop at each wire end.

BLACK CRYSTAL BRACELET

SHOPPING LIST

- ☐ memory wire
- ☐ assorted small, medium, and large black crystal bicone beads (we used approx. 85 beads)
- ☐ silver heart beads (we used 7)
- ☐ silver head pins
- ☐ memory wire shears
- ☐ wire cutters, chain-nose pliers (2 pair) and round-nose pliers

To make the Bracelet:

1. Wrap the memory wire around your wrist 2-3 times to determine bracelet length. Use the memory wire shears to cut a piece of wire this length. Make a loop at one wire end (page 32).

2. Thread the beads on the wire as desired. Make a loop at the remaining wire end.

3. Use the heart beads and head pins to make 2 bead dangles (page 32). Attach a bead dangle to the loop at each wire end.

Neon Knots

PUZZLE CHARM BRACELET

SHOPPING LIST

- ☐ bangle bracelet with removable ends
- ☐ 2mm satin cord
- ☐ 12 puzzle charms with attached jump rings
- ☐ craft glue

To make the Bracelet:

1. Remove the ball from one bracelet end.
2. Cut a 72" cord length. Fold the cord in half and tie the cord center to the ball end of the bracelet. Tie 2 square knots (page 32) around the bracelet. Slide on a charm. Tie 2 more square knots.
3. Continue adding charms and tying 2 square knots until you reach the end of the bracelet. Wrap the cords ends to the wrong side of the bracelet and glue in place. When the glue is dry, replace the ball on the bracelet.

BEADED BRACELETS

SHOPPING LIST

- ☐ braiding cord
- ☐ assorted 8mm round beads (we used 14 for each bracelet)

To make each Bracelet:

1. Cut three 36" cord lengths.
2. Holding the cord pieces together at one end, tie an overhand knot (page 32) about 3" from the end. Tape the knot down.
3. Use the 2 outer cords to tie 4 square knots (page 32) around the center cord. Slide a bead on the center cord and tie another square knot.
4. Continue adding beads and tying square knots until the bracelet is 3/4" short of the desired length. Tie 3 more square knots. Tie an overhand knot close to the last square knot. Trim the cord ends about 3" from the overhand knot.

Safety Pin Necklace & Bracelet

NECKLACE

SHOPPING LIST

- ☐ $1^1/_8$" coil-less safety pins (we used 9)
- ☐ assorted pre-made small charms and bead dangles (we used 9)
- ☐ assorted seed beads (we used 127)
- ☐ chain necklace with an add-a-bead-clasp

To make the Necklace:

1. Slide 6-7 seed beads, a charm **or** bead dangle, and another 6-7 seed beads on each safety pin; close the pin *(Fig. 1)*.

Fig. 1

2. Beginning and ending with a seed bead, alternately thread the beaded safety pins and seed beads on the necklace.

BRACELET

SHOPPING LIST

- ☐ $1^1/_8$" safety pins (we used 32 for a 7" long bracelet)
- ☐ assorted seed, bugle, and cube beads
- ☐ assorted 6/0 beads (you'll need 2 more than the number of safety pins you use)
- ☐ stretch cord
- ☐ jeweler's glue
- ☐ flexible wire beading needle (optional)
- ☐ chain-nose pliers

To make the Bracelet:

1. Slide 3-6 assorted seed/bugle/cube beads on each safety pin; close the pin *(Fig. 1)*.

Fig. 1

2. Use the pliers to tightly close and then flatten the catch end of each pin *(Figs. 2-3)*.

Fig. 2

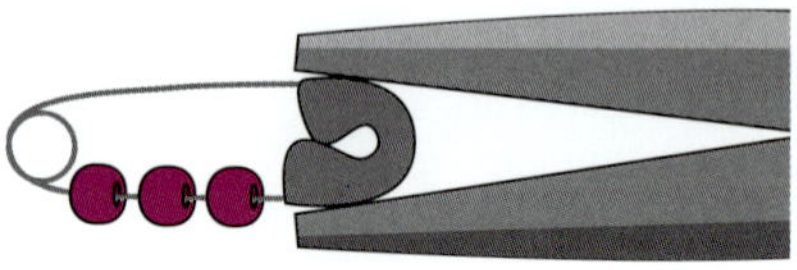

Fig. 3

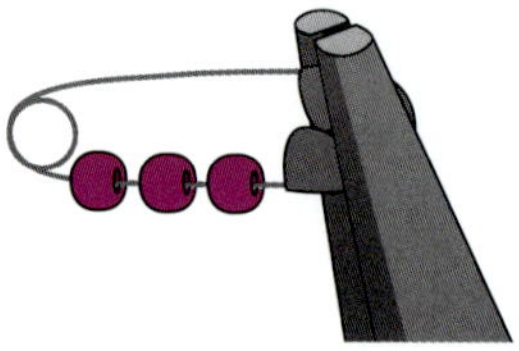

3. Cut two 12" lengths of cord. Place a bead stop at one end of each cord. Spacing the cords 1" apart, tape down the cords. Keeping the cords parallel as you work, alternately thread 6/0 beads and beaded safety pins on the cords *(Fig. 4)*.

4. Check the bracelet size, adding or removing beads and safety pins until the bracelet is the desired length. Remove the bead stops. Tie the cord ends with a surgeon's knot *(Fig. 5)* and apply a drop of glue to each knot. Once dry, trim the cord ends.

Fig. 4

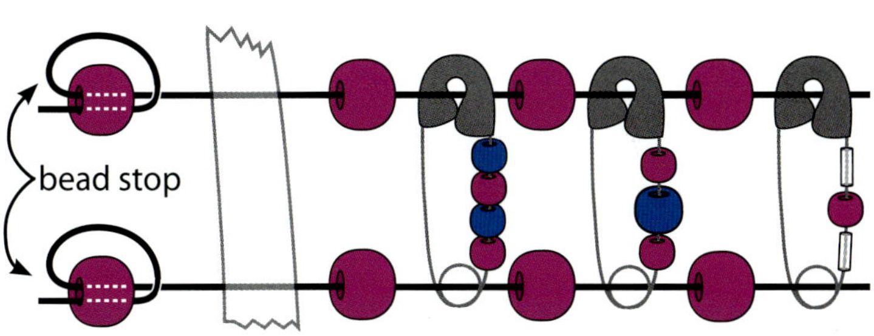

Fig. 5

Wood & Chain Necklace & Bracelet

This eye-catching set begins with a pre-beaded chain and a pre-made chain necklace which allows you to create these fabulous jewelry pieces that will amaze your friends. While this project may appear to be more challanging than some, your friends never have to know just how easy it really was!

SHOPPING LIST

- ☐ wood seed beads on a jump ring chain
- ☐ pre-made 16" long antique brass chain necklace
- ☐ antique brass pendant
- ☐ brown braiding cord
- ☐ antique brass lobster clasp
- ☐ large antique brass jump rings
- ☐ 1 antique brass head pin
- ☐ 4 beads (we used an extra large, large, medium, and small bead)
- ☐ wire cutters
- ☐ chain-nose pliers (2 pair) and round-nose pliers
- ☐ craft glue

To make the Necklace:

1. Open and remove the chain link (page 31) at the center of the necklace.

2. Cut two 20" cord lengths. Fold a cord in half and insert the ends through the first chain link on the necklace. Alternately going around and through the links, weave both cord ends through the links of the necklace ***(Fig. 1)***.

Fig. 1

3. When you reach the clasp, securely knot the cord ends. Apply a drop of glue to the knot and allow to dry; clip the cord ends close to the knot. Repeat on the other side of the necklace with the remaining cord piece.

4. Cut two 7" long pieces of wood seed bead chain. Place the chains side-by-side. Join the 2 pieces at each end with a jump ring ***(Fig. 2)***.

Fig. 2

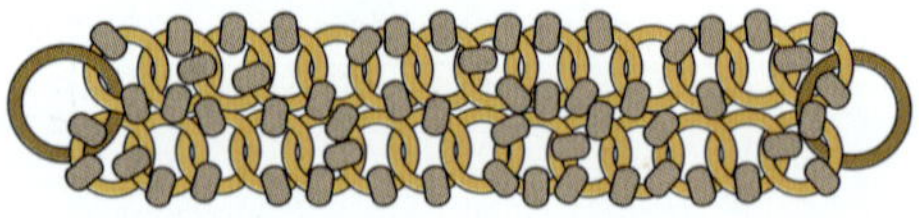

5. Join the beaded chain to the necklace with the attached jump rings ***(Fig. 3)***. Attach the pendant to the center of the beaded chain with a jump ring.

Fig. 3

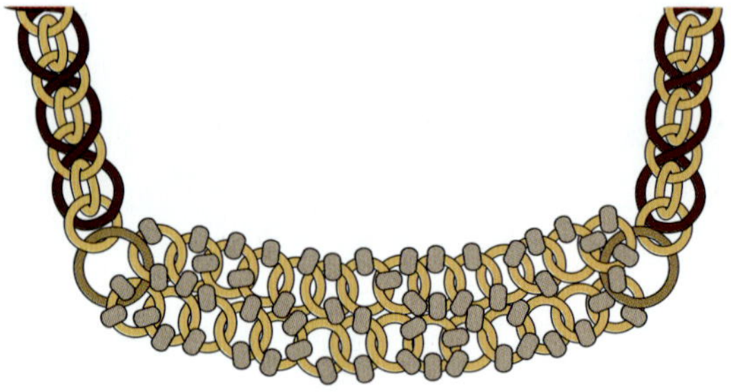

Continued on page 24.

To make the bracelet:

1. Cut a piece of wood seed bead chain that is twice the desired finished length. Cut a piece of cord the determined length plus 4".

2. Fold the beaded chain in half and attach a jump ring at the fold; attach the clasp to the jump ring ***(Fig. 4)***.

Fig. 4

3. Fold the cord in half and insert the ends through the 2 beaded jump rings closest to the clasp. Crossing at the center, weave the cords from back and forth between the beaded chains ***(Fig. 5)***.

Fig. 5

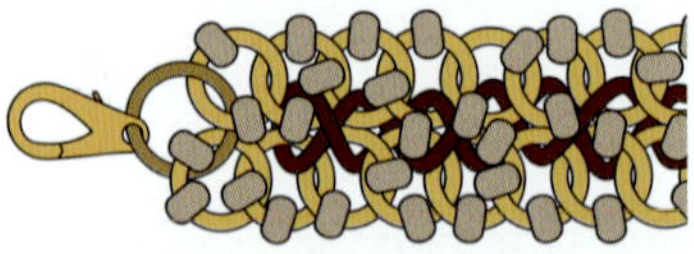

4. When you reach the end of the chains, securely knot the cord ends. Apply a drop of glue to the knot and allow to dry; clip the cord ends close to the knot. Attach the chain ends to a jump ring ***(Fig. 6)***.

Fig. 6

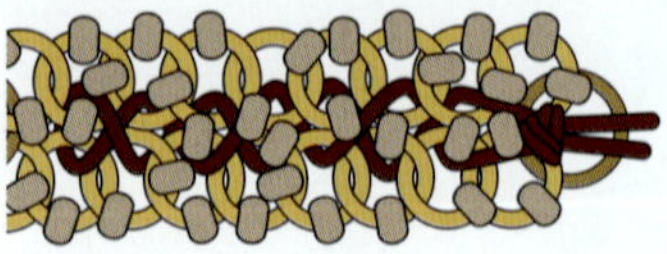

5. Make a bead dangle (page 32) with the beads and head pin. Attach the bead dangle to the center of the bracelet with a jump ring.

Twelve Days of Earrings

Just visit the jewelry section of any craft store and you can't help being inspired by the huge selection of beads and findings available. Earrings are a fast and easy way to experiment with different materials, textures and colors. With just a few simple techniques, supplies, and tools you can create a whole wardrobe of earrings to suit your every mood.

The photos on the right are for inspiration; the shopping list below includes the basic items you will need to get started. The techniques for making bead dangles, making connectors, and using jump rings begin on page 31.

SHOPPING LIST

- ☐ assorted beads (we used glass, metal, stone, and plastic)
- ☐ assorted charms
- ☐ assorted jump rings (we used round and square)
- ☐ assorted ear wires and hoops
- ☐ head pins
- ☐ eye pins
- ☐ wire cutters
- ☐ chain-nose pliers (2 pair) and round-nose pliers

Slip a glass bead inside a metal ring
Use glass & rhinestone beads to make dangles on decorative head pins
Include some fun & flirty pre-made connectors

Use square jump rings to add interest to single bead dangles
Slip pre-made charms & bead dangles on silver hoops
Add bead dangles to pendants
Add length with a connector
Attach a bead dangle

Large-Hole Bead Jewelry

BRACELET, NECKLACE & EARRINGS

The projects on page 29 are oh-so-easy to make when you combine pre-made findings with assorted large-hole beads and spacers. Just slide beads on your chosen findings and—instant jewelry!

You can use the shopping list, below, for suggestions and inspiration when looking for components for your jewelry pieces. You will be amazed at all the pre-made findings available!

SHOPPING LIST

- ☐ chain necklaces and bracelets
- ☐ satin cord necklaces and bracelets
- ☐ snake-style add-a-bead necklaces and bracelets
- ☐ metal bangle-style bracelets with removable ball ends
- ☐ hoop earrings
- ☐ assorted large-hole, metal-lined glass, crystal, and rhinestone beads
- ☐ assorted large-hole metal beads and spacers

SATIN CORD BRACELET

Shown on page 30

SHOPPING LIST

- ☐ 2mm satin cord
- ☐ 1 large-hole metal-lined bead
- ☐ 4 large-hole faceted beads
- ☐ 2 large-hole rhinestone spacer beads
- ☐ 2 metal silver knot spacer beads

To make the Bracelet:

1. Cut two 24" cord lengths. Tape the center of the cords to a work surface *(Fig. 1)*.

2. Slide the metal-lined bead and the 2 rhinestone spacer beads to the center of the cords, just below the tape *(Fig. 2)*.

Fig. 1

Fig. 2

Continued on page 30.

Large-Hole Bead Jewelry Continued.

3. Crossing the cords inside the bead, slide a faceted bead onto the cords ***(Fig. 3)***.

4. Repeat Step 3 to add a metal bead and another faceted bead. Tie an overhand knot just below the last bead to complete one side of the bracelet ***(Fig. 4)***.

5. For the remaining side, remove the tape and repeat Steps 3-4. Trim the cord ends.

Fig. 3

Fig. 4

General Instructions

TOOLS

Chain-nose pliers have rounded, tapered jaws and a flat interior surface that will not mar wire. These pliers are used for reaching into tight places, gripping objects, opening and closing jump rings, and bending wire.

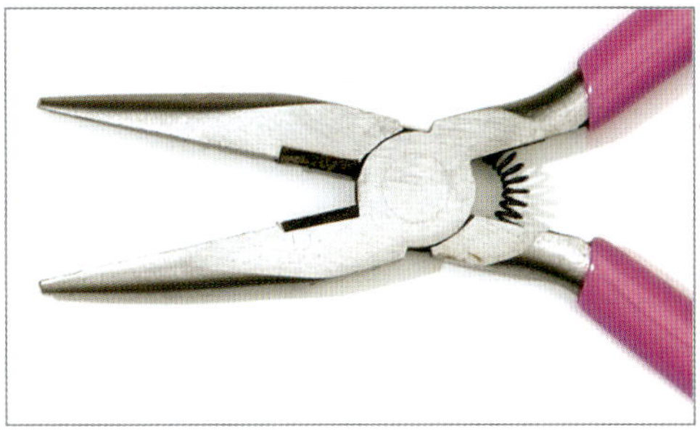

Round-nose pliers have round jaws that are useful for making loops and bending wire smoothly.

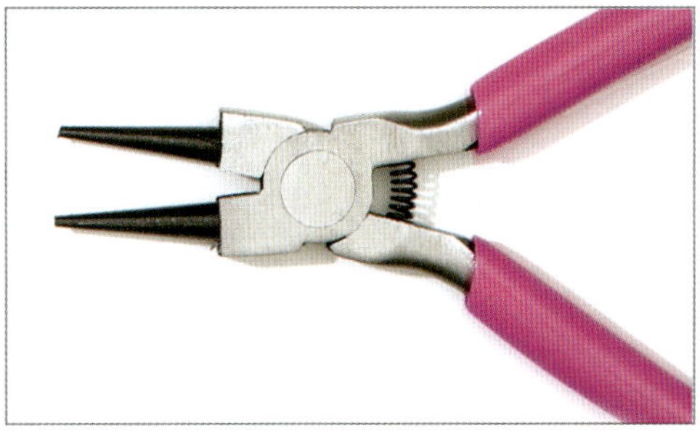

Wire cutters are used to cut small gauge wire, head pins, and eye pins.

TECHNIQUES

Opening and Closing Jump Rings, Chain Links, and Loops on Eye Pins or Head Pins

Pick up a jump ring with chain-nose pliers. With a second pair of chain-nose pliers, gently hold the other side of the ring. Open the ring by pulling one pair of pliers toward you while pushing the other away *(Fig. 1)*.

Fig. 1

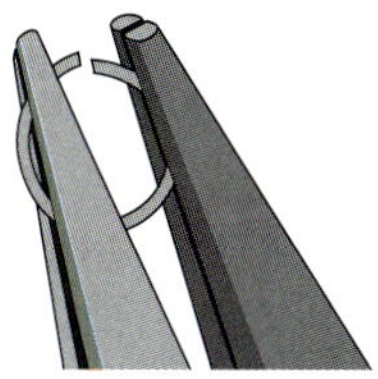

Close the ring by pushing and pulling the pliers in opposite directions, bringing the ring ends back together. Open and close chain links and loops on eye pins or head pins the same way.

Attaching Foldover Cord Ends

Place the necklace ends in the foldover cord ends and add a drop of glue. Use chain-nose pliers to close the tabs *(Fig. 2)*.

Fig. 2

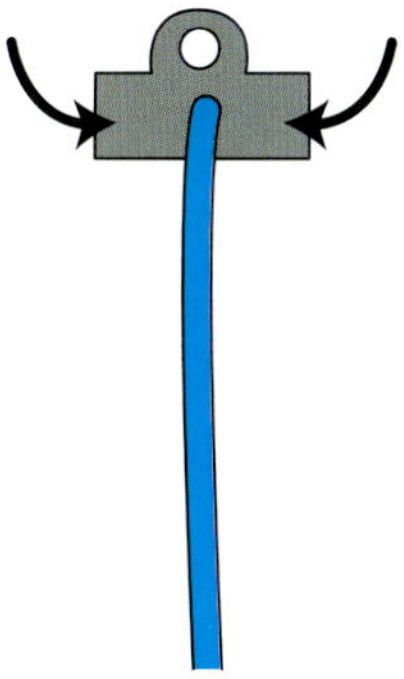

Making a Bead Dangle, Connector, or Loops on Wire

Bead Dangles are made on head pins and have a loop at one end. Connectors are made on eye pins and have loops on both ends. Loops on wire ends are made in the same manner as the loops on bead dangles and connectors.

Slide the beads on a head pin or eye pin. Leaving about 1/2", cut off the excess wire. Using chain-nose pliers, bend the wire at a 90° angle *(Fig. 3)*. Grasp the wire end with the round-nose pliers. Turn the pliers and bend the wire into a loop *(Fig. 4)*. Release the pliers. Straighten or twist the loop further if necessary.

Fig. 3

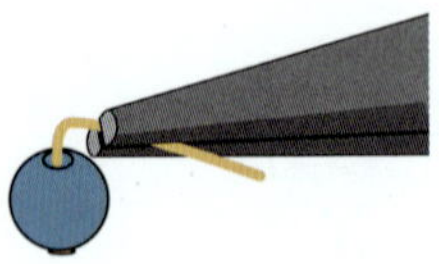

Fig. 4

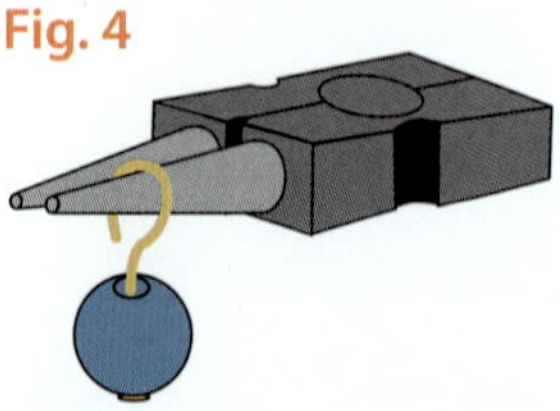

Tying an Overhand Knot

Hold the cords together and tie an overhand knot *(Fig. 5)* near one end.

Fig. 5

Tying a Square Knot

Use the outer cords to tie the first half of a square knot around the center cord or cords *(Fig. 6)*.

Fig. 6

Use the outer cords to tie the second half of a square knot *(Fig. 7)*.

Fig.7

Production Team: Crafts Design Director – Patti Wallenfang; Designer – Kelly Reider; Technical Writer – Jean Lewis; Technical Associate – Mary Sullivan Hutcheson; Editorial Writer – Susan Frantz Wiles; Senior Graphic Artist – Lora Puls; Graphic Artist – Jessica Bramlett and Cailen Cochran; Photostylist – Lori Wenger; Photographers – Jason Masters and Ken West.